Winning In Traffic Court

Winning in Traffic Court
© 2003 Seymour Stern
Miami, Florida
www.winning-in-traffic-court.com

CONTENTS

INTRODUCTION

Most people ticketed for a traffic infraction accept that costly fines, points against their license and an increase in the monthly insurance premium, are inevitable.

The reason for this mistaken belief is a lack of knowledge of:

- Traffic laws
- Court rules and regulations
- Defenses to a specific infraction
- Tactics and strategies for how the system can be used to increase the states burden to prove guilt.

In this book, you will learn how to have your case dismissed using only legal tactics and rules of evidence.

Even a driver who did violate a traffic law is not *guilty* of violating that traffic law until there has been a full and complete hearing before the court wherein sufficient, credible and competent evidence has been produced by the state for the court to make a finding of guilt. Until such time, the law presumes the accused to be innocent and not guilty.

Therefore, were you in fact speeding beyond the posted speed limit? Answer: "yes".

Are you guilty of speeding? Answer: "no"… Not until a court finds you guilty.

This booklet outlines the evidence, in documents and testimony, which the state must produce in order for the court to find a driver guilty of violating a traffic law.

Guilt or innocence of a traffic offender is the end result of a process that requires the state to prove guilt beyond a reasonable doubt. *Fla. Statute 318.14(6)*.

The accused never has to prove innocence since it is the state's burden to prove guilt. The accused need only listen to the state's case against him and then move to dismiss the case in the event the state has failed to prove each and every element that comprises the offense. The accused need not even offer a defense to the infraction if the state fails to make out a *prima facie* case.

The information contained in this booklet is applicable to the laws of the State of Florida, but because traffic infraction laws are so similar from state to state, the defense tactics and strategies are generally applicable to other state laws. However it is best to review the specific law the driver is accused of violating. This is can be done very simply and sometimes without leaving your home.

Traffic offenses are divided into two categories: civil and criminal. Because of the complexity and seriousness of a traffic criminal offense, this booklet covers only civil infractions. It is recommended that the services of an attorney experienced in criminal traffic cases be retained for defense of the charge.

HOW TO HANDLE AN INFRACTION STOP

Winning in traffic court begins when the blue lights flash and the siren sounds. The natural reaction is surprise, apprehension and anxiety, but these emotions can disturb your composure and affect your self-control. The ability for you to control the events after a stop is crucial to the defense in court.

If you are pulled over, a ticket is probably heading your way, so let's control events at the start and win in court later. After all, if you are not *in* control then you are *out* of control.

Keeping the officer calm and not apprehensive is the goal of control. Do your best to give him/her no reason to remember you. Many officers have lost their lives during a routine traffic stop and they are naturally apprehensive. Remember to do the following when stopped:

- Stop in a safe area and out of traffic.

- Roll down the window and have your license and registration ready to hand to the officer. Don't wait to be asked for it.

- If it's dark, <u>turn on the dome light</u> so the officer can see you.

- Place both hands on the wheel.

- Do not attempt to get out of the vehicle.

- If you are wearing dark sunglasses, remove them.

The officer will immediately recognize your behavior as non-aggressive. Being cooperative may go a long way in a ticket not being issued.

STEP ONE: Don't admit your guilt

A common question asked by officers is, "Do you know why I stopped you?"

This is an invitation for you to admit guilt, which will be duly noted and testified to at the hearing. A benign answer, such as " I honestly don't know" or "I guess you know better than I do," is best. The officer will take notes of everything said at the stop, including any admissions by you, so say as little as possible. Trying to talk your way out of the ticket is usually useless and (unless you have a *very* good excuse) can actually make the matter even worse by inflaming the situation.

> An important aspect of taking control is to be very polite, respectful and to answer all questions directly.

The officer will take your license and registration back to his/her patrol car where the ticket will be issued and a routine check of your license plate is completed. The officer will then return to your vehicle, hand you the citation and ask you to sign his copy. **Refusal to sign the copy is a misdemeanor in the second degree and you are subject to immediate arrest.** *Fla. Statute 318.14(3).*

Signing the copy is your promise to appear in court at the appropriate time and place and your failure to do so can result in a warrant issued by the court for your arrest.

While the officer is writing the ticket, take the time to note the time and place of the stop and record, in writing, roadway and traffic conditions, weather and any other fact that is relevant to the alleged offense.
The officer may ask to search the vehicle and if allowed may find reason to write additional tickets. This could include finding open alcohol containers or perhaps discovering other more serious reasons for an arrest. A search is not legally permitted without an order of the court unless there is observable probable cause for the officer to justify the search.

Never become argumentative, wave your arms, raise your voice; use physical body language; use inappropriate language or do anything else to get the officer angry or upset. Doing this is playing his game; he wins; you lose.

Winning in traffic court is accomplished in the courtroom, not curbside.

THE TRAFFIC TICKET

The traffic ticket is also called a citation and its informational content, if used correctly, can effectively be your best defense. The ticket will state the offense in general terms such as "exceeding the speed limit" but will also specify the section of law by a state statute number that legally defines the traffic offense by statutory elements that comprise the offense.

It is the statute number that defines the offense and not the general language on the ticket. There is sometimes a difference between the general language and the statute number. If the statute number that describes the offense is different than the offense for which you were stopped and you are tried on that erroneous charge that charge can be dismissed and you cannot be tried on the original correct charge. This is based on the law of double jeopardy that does not allow a person to be tried twice.

The statute cited on the citation defines and describes the offense in elements that totally comprise the offense. These statutory elements determine the state's burden of proof to find guilt. The state must offer acceptable evidence on each and every element that is described in the statute. Missing just one element makes the state's case dismissible for failure to prove a *prima facie* case.

Prima facie means that the party having the burden of proof (the state, in traffic cases) must present sufficient and credible evidence one each and every element that is described in the statute. Missing just one element makes the state's case dismissible for failure to prove a prima facie case.

If the officer fails to offer evidence on each and every element and the state has rested its case, the accused can then call the court's attention to the missing elements and request the court to dismiss the case on the basis that the state has failed to prove a *prima facie* case.

The citation will name the location of the court where the ticket is returnable, meaning where the hearing will take place. The accused has a right to request the court to change the location of the hearing to the court at the county seat as long as a sufficient reason is given to the court. In legal terminology this is called a change of venue.

Sufficient reason can be that your home and work are closer to the county seat court and that witnesses you intend to call on your behalf also live and work nearer to the county seat court. You can state that your ability to present a defense will be jeopardized if your witnesses are unable to appear.

This change of venue can be accomplished sometimes by a phone call to the traffic court clerk or with a simple letter to the clerk. The strategy of changing venue is that it will place an additional burden upon the officer to appear and testify. He/she must appear or the ticket will be dismissed.

Requesting a change in the hearing date based upon your prior commitments (either personal or business or both) or for health reasons or for witness appearances will have the same effect of increasing the chance the officer will not appear because of a change in his schedule or work assignment. It is important to remember that both you and the court must be absolutely clear when and where the hearing will occur. Your failure to appear at the hearing is cause for a warrant to be issued for your arrest. *(Fla Traffic.Rule 6.190.)*

The citation will give you an option to plead guilty to the offense and pay a predetermined fine by mail. The court will also give you the option to attend traffic school in lieu of a court appearance. *(Fla. Rules of Traffic Court 6.330 and Fla. Statute 318.14(9).)*

The benefits of choosing traffic school include:

- No points will be assessed against the license.
- There is no finding or adjudication of guilt.
- Insurance rates will not increase because there will be no adjudication of guilt.
- The fine will be decreased by 18%

The arrangement for traffic school can be made with the court clerk as well as payment of the fine. There is no need for a court appearance. Traffic school is not available if it has been exercised within the previous twelve months.

You also have a legal right to a speedy trial. This means the state must try the case within a specified period of time, usually 180 days from the date of the offense. The case must be dismissed if it is not heard in court within that time. However, if you cause a delay for any reason the speedy trial rule does not apply (Fla. Rules of Traffic Court 6.325).

ELEMENTS AND EVIDENCE

The statute number appearing on the citation is the charge against the offender, and the statute describes the offense in or by various elements. This means that the statute sets forth the offense in separate allegations that taken together describes the offense. These separate allegations are the elements of the offense.

The elements of the offense become your best friend, your best defense, and the heart of the trial strategy and tactic. Guilt or innocence is really not the issue in defending a traffic case, although it is the end result. The real issue is whether the state has made out a *prima facie* case by introducing acceptable and competent evidence on each and every element to convince the court you actually committed the acts that comprise the offense. Again, the state has the burden to prove every element of the offense. Failure to prove just one element is sufficient cause for the case to be dismissed. There is no such thing in the law as partial guilt.

Finding the statute number noted on the citation.

Finding the statute is as easy as booting up the home or office computer and logging into the state statutes. If this cannot be accomplished a visit to the local court library will suffice. Court librarians are very courteous and helpful in locating the statute you seek. Copy machines are generally available for a small fee, and you will not need more than one page. If you have the time and inclination there are also cases that show how the court decided in similar cases.

Once you have found the statute that describes the offense you should do the following:

- Read it very carefully and make a copy

- Separate the elements by writing each one on a sheet of paper.

You will know from reading the statute and its elements exactly what the state must prove in acceptable evidence to make out a prima facie case.

Example one of separating elements

If you were accused of "careless driving" in Florida the citation would list state statute 316.1925 as the offense committed. At this point you will also know if the officer wrote the incorrect statute number on the citation. Statute 316.1925 defining careless driving will read as follows:

> *Any person operating a motor vehicle upon the streets or highways within the state shall drive the same in a careful and prudent manner having regard for the width/ grade/ curves/ corners/ traffic and all other attendant circumstances so as not to endanger the life/ limb/ or property of any person. Failure to drive in such a manner shall constitute careless driving and a violation of this section.*

This statute has four elements that the state must prove to make out a prima facie case:

- The violation must occur on a street or highway and not on private property such as a supermarket parking lot or other private property

- The vehicle must be driven in a manner not prudent. (Prudent means using good judgment).

- The driver disregarded the width, grade, curve and comer of the road, its traffic

- Persons or property, life and limb must have been endangered

Failure to prove anyone of these elements is fatal to the state's case.

Example number two of separating elements:

The offense of "following too closely" is described in Florida State statute 316. 0895 and reads as follows:

> *The driver of a motor vehicle shall not follow another vehicle more closely than is/ reasonable/ and prudent/ having regard for the speed / of such vehicle and the /traffic upon/ and the condition of the highway.*

The elements the state must prove for a conviction are:

- The driver drove in an unreasonable manner.

  Unreasonable has such broad and wide interpretation that it means different things to different people. The state must wrestle

14

with what unreasonable means as it relates to a traffic offense of following too closely.

- The driver was not prudent in the operation of the vehicle

- The state must prove the speed of the vehicle that was being followed

Traffic is an element that the state must factor into the offense as it relates to following too closely

Condition of the highway must be a factor in finding guilt as it relates to the offense.

Whenever a statute uses words that have a wide and broad meaning, it makes the state's case more difficult to prove.

THE SPEEDING INFRACTION

The speeding infraction ticket is probable the most often issued ticket by cities and towns for revenue purposes.

Speeding fines generate the most cost-effective revenue and can easily cost upwards of several hundred dollars. *Fla. Statute 318.18(3) (a)*. The state allows each municipality to regulate the speed of vehicles within its jurisdiction. *Fla. Statute 316.189*.

This is the basis for certain towns or cities to be labeled "speed traps" by automobile associations and television shows, thereby exposing towns that use traffic fines solely for the purpose of increasing revenue.

Florida Statute 316.187 requires the Department of Transportation to set speeds based upon an engineering and traffic investigation to determine what speed is greater or less than is reasonable upon a highway outside a municipality.

This statute is significant on a citation issued for speeding. Speeding convictions have been reversed where the state failed to show that the statute imposing the speed limit was based on an investigation.

Every speeding ticket is grounded in the use of a speed measuring device with the exception of an officer who issued the ticket strictly on visual estimate of speed, a very rare occasion.

The device is usually a speedometer in the officer's patrol car, a radar unit, a vascar recorder or a laser unit. Each device is treated separately with defenses outlined for that specific device as well as tactics and strategy.

Understanding how these devices operate, as well as understanding their limitations and the ability of the officer to use the device, is crucial to defending a charge of speeding.

The most often issued ticket for speeding is also the easiest to defend (sometimes without even offering a defense to the charge) because the state has set extremely high standards of proof and expertise by the officer using the device. These high standards and burdens the state must meet do not come into play unless the accused forces the state to meet that burden.

Each state enacts its own speed laws and the concept of what constitutes a finding of guilt for speeding varies in certain states. Some states have a speed standard referred to as "presumed speed" and some "absolute speed." The difference is significant because the defense is different for each.

A state that adopts the "presumed speed" allows a violator who has exceeded the posted speed to admit the excessive speed but defend on the grounds that the speed, although above the limit, was safe for traffic, highway and weather conditions and no persons were endangered at the time the offense occurred.

In states that adopt the "absolute speed" concept, such as Florida, even one mile per hour over the posted speed limit is sufficient for a finding of guilt and the safe speed defense is not allowed.

The defense to the absolute speed limit considers:

- The competence of the officer to use the device

- The required periodic testing of the device

How the device was tested as well as the accuracy of the device and documents that must be produced by the officer at the hearing.

Determining speed is accomplished by various methods such as visual speed, speedometer; radar, laser, vascar and photo speed radar.

Visual speed estimate: the officer determines speed by eye. This is a very inaccurate method and generally speeding tickets are not issued on this basis because the following points are all subject to question and interpretation:

- how long the officer observed the vehicle
- over what distance
- his/her angle of vision
- the curvature of the road
- the officers ability to measure speed by eye
- his/her history of accuracy of speed over a measured distance

Clearly this is not an accurate method to determine speed of a vehicle.

Speedometer: this method requires the officer in a patrol car to follow the speeding vehicle:

- for a sufficient distance
- at the same speed
- without varying the distance between the vehicles

Any of these things will affect the speed that is determined. Upgrades, downgrades and curves in the road will have an effect on determining speed. Once the officer determines the speed by reading his speedometer, the accuracy of his/her speedometer becomes a major issue in proving guilt; and the burden is upon the state to prove accuracy provided the accused raises the issue. Failure of the accused to do so makes it the word of the officer over the accused. For a speedometer to be determined accurate, it is legally required to be tested every six months by a speedometer shop registered with the Florida Department of Agriculture and Consumer Services and a certificate issued by the authorized person to test the speedometer; witnessed and dated. *(Florida Admin.. Code Rule 15H- 2.011 of the Department of Highway Safety and Motor Vehicles.)*

If the test date does not occur within six months of the offense the test cannot be used as evidence of accuracy of the speedometer.

Florida law is very specific about the use of electrical, mechanical or other speed calculating devices. Florida Statute 316.1905 limits their use as follows: the device must be approved by the Department of Highway Safety and Motor Vehicles and shall have been tested to determine that it is operating accurately. Tests for this purpose shall be made not less than every six months according to procedures and at regular intervals of time prescribed by the Department of Highway Safety and Motor Vehicles.

RADAR SPEEDING
INFRACTIONS

Radar speeding infraction tickets are issued more than any other infraction. The reason is that radar speeding infractions produce the greatest revenue in the most cost- effective way. Most drivers think a radar speeding offense is impossible to beat because radar has been accepted for many years as a scientifically proven device and especially when a police officer is ready to testify to back up the device. However the courts have found radar to be unreliable scientifically to determine speed.

In the landmark case of State vs. Aquilera 48 Fla. Supp. 207 Judge Alfred Nesbitt found after extensive testimony by experts that radar has inherent errors and listed them as follows: "Cosine error; Batching error; Panning and Scanning errors; Shadowing errors; errors due to outside interference such as billboards, overpasses, passing C .B. radios and many other similar causes; errors due to inside interference such as heaters and air conditioning fans, and police radios etc; errors due to improper mounting of the radar unit; errors due to heat buildup; errors due to power surge by shutting off and turning on the radar at the last minute to avoid radar detecting devices; errors due to the auto lock system; errors due to reliance on the auto alarm system; errors due to the mirror switch aiming; and errors in the identification of target vehicles due to the modem day traffic patterns and the mixture of size of vehicles and varied materials in their construction."

The court went on to state, "Let it be understood once and for all, the function of the traffic court is to convict the guilty, acquit the innocent, and improve traffic safety, not to be merely an arm of any revenue collection office."

The court then issued its decision: "Based upon all of the testimony, exhibits, and arguments of counsel, I find that the reliability of the radar speed measuring devices as used in their present modes and particularly in these cases, has not been established beyond and to the exclusion of every reasonable doubt, nor has it met the test of reasonable scientific certainty, and it is therefore ordered and adjudged that the motions to suppress and/or exclude herein be and they are hereby granted".

By understanding what the state must produce in documentary and oral evidence, the accused can use the law to his advantage and the state's disadvantage. But this does not happen unless the accused objects to any deviation by the state of its burden of proof and most advise the judge that the state's evidence is not admissible or does not meet the law's requirements. The burden is upon the accused to object to any evidence not meeting the statutory standard because the judge will allow almost anything into the court record unless a party objects.

Because radar is subject to erroneous speed displays caused by radio frequency interference (RFI) and many other reasons the law requires radar units to be equipped with a RF sensor capable of detecting the presence of such interfering RF signals and of inhibiting any speed display when such signals are present. *Department of Highway Safety and Motor Vehicles 15B-2.0081(10). Fla. Admin. Code*

It should be noted that the state statutes governing traffic violations and its rules and regulations are only part of the law because the Florida Administrative Code also controls traffic infractions by their own administrative laws. What constitutes the law is the totality of all the laws. What constitutes the law is the totality of all the laws that bear on traffic offenses. Therefore the accused has another set of laws that can be used to lawfully increase the states burden to prove guilt; especially in radar speed cases. By understanding these laws and applying them an accused can have the case dismissed without even testifying or even offering any evidence of innocence.

Not only is the radar device unreliable, but certain pre-conditions for its use by the officer must be proven by the state. The officer who operated the device must meet rigid tests before, during and after its use. Unless and until all these legal requirements and precautions are validly proven by competent and admissible evidence, the state has failed to prove a prima facie case.

The state in a radar speeding infraction offense must prove by competent admissible evidence the following:

1.   The operator of the device (the police officer) has satisfactorily completed the radar-training course established by the Criminal Justice Standards and Training Commission. *Fla .Statute 316.1906 and Fl. Administrative Code 15B-2.007(2).*

It is not sufficient for the officer to orally say he completed the course but a Certificate of the satisfactory completion of the course must be offered and accepted into the record. Failure to do so is sufficient to move the court to dismiss the case. Florida Statute 943.17(1)(b) and the cases *State vs. Bender 382 So.2d 697* and *State vs. Potter 438 So.2d 1085* requires such evidence as a prerequisite to the officer's testimony. The number behind the name of the case signifies where that particular case can be found. Number 382 means it is the 382nd volume published in the Southern 2nd series and the last number 1085 is the page of that volume.

2. "The officer has to make an independent visual determination that the vehicle is operating in excess of the applicable speed limit". But this requirement is also subject to what the officer must have viewed when the vehicle was in motion for a sufficient length of time to be able to formulate a judgment as to its speed. If he didn't, then his judgment is not legally acceptable. The visual observation of the vehicle's speed is secondary to the radar and if the radar case is dismissed the visual observation cannot be used as evidence of speed. This is a requirement under section 316.1906 Florida Statutes.

3. The officer "has written a citation based on evidence obtained from radar when conditions permit the clear assignment of speed to a single vehicle". This means the officer as part of the State's *prima facie* case must testify that based on the radar's finding of excessive speed relates to the offender's vehicle, and none other. His failure to so testify renders the case dismissible.

4. The officer must testify he/she was operating the radar "which had no automatic speed locks and no audio alarms, unless disconnected or deactivated. "An auto lock or auto alarm enables the officer to set

the radar unit for a certain speed. When a vehicle enters the radar field exceeding that speed limit, an alarm goes off and the speed is locked into the digital read-out screen. Unless the officer so testifies the speed lock or alarm was not activated the State has not met its burden of proof.

5.   The officer must testify that he/she was operating the radar unit with "audio Doppler engaged." Audio Doppler means a back -up audible signal that translates the radar's Doppler shift into a tone, which can be heard by the radar operator.

6.   The officer must produce a document that he/she was using radar "which meets the minimum design criteria for such units established by the Department of Highway Safety and Motor Vehicles." This means the officer must first identify by serial number of manufacturer or some other reliable information the radar unit he/she was using and produce a document that the unit meets the design criteria. Rule 15B-2.0082 Fla. Admin Code sets forth the specific standards by reference that the unit must meet.

7.   The officer must produce a certificate or document that the radar unit used was approved by the Department of Highway Safety and Motor Vehicles/ Section 316.1905(1). The document must be a certified letter from that department.

8.   The officer must testify and produce a certificate or document that the unit used was tested within the previous six months of the citation issued and found to be functioning correctly. In addition the document must contain the following information; the certificate must be signed and witnessed by the

examiner; the unit must be bench tested, meaning it had to be removed from the patrol car and tested at an electrical laboratory or shop; the examiner must have a current and proper FCC license within the six month period. Unless the certificate meets these statutory requirements the certificate cannot be accepted into evidence and used against the offender. Since the certificate is one of the essential proofs necessary to find guilt the case is dismissible for failure of the state to make out a *prima facie* case.

9.   In addition to the above requirements the officer must produce a "written log" demonstrating that specified internal and external accuracy tuning fork checks of the device were performed by the officer both before and after each citation was issued for speeding. Further, the log forms must be of a design suitable to the needs of the operator's jurisdiction. The internal accuracy test is passed only if the proper numbers recommended by the manufacturer appear exactly on the radar screen. The external tuning fork accuracy check must be made with certified tuning forks (plus or minus one mile per hour tolerance) furnished by the manufacturer. *Fl. Admin. Code Rule 15B-2.009 and the case Tegnelia vs. State of Florida 23 Fla. Supp.2d 149.*

The method of using the above necessary testimony and production of documents or certificates in a radar speeding case is to simply make a list of the necessary documents and a list of the required testimony that the State must prove and check off the ones that are met. What is left unchecked is the proof required but not met, and therefore the state has failed to meet its evidentiary requirements and the case is dismissible for failure to make out a *prima facie* case. **Then you win, the State loses.**

After the officer has completed his/her testimony and offered whatever documents were accepted into evidence the first question to ask the officer as part of your cross examination is " Officer, did you bring any documents, certificates or writings of any kind or nature besides the ones you have already introduced?"

If the answer is "no" you can then ask him to produce those documents he hasn't produced and when he doesn't produce them, it is in the courts record and the judge is aware of the state's failure to produce. This is the legal basis for a motion, by you to the court to dismiss the case.

A motion, in non-legal jargon simply means you are asking the court to either do something or to not do something. When a document is produced, take the time to examine it carefully to see if it meets all the requirements and if not, object to it being accepted into evidence because it did not meet the statutory requirements.

This is the legal way of using the law and the rules of evidence to force the state to meet its legal burden of proof or lose the case.

TRAFFIC INFRACTION
BY VASCAR

Vascar is short hand for Visual Average Speed Computer Devices. A quarter mile is measured off and when a vehicle enters the measured distance a computer device with a self-contained time base records the time it took the vehicle to cover the distance and converts the time to MPH. Again, the accuracy of the device is vital to proving guilt.

The state requires verification of the device each day before and after citations are issued. The results of the verification must be recorded and retained for future reference. *Fla. Admin. Code 15B-2.0101.*

If the verification is recorded there is a document that must be produced to prove accuracy. The operator of a vascar device must pass a field test and a certificate produced in court to prove compliance with this requirement.

TRAFFIC INFRACTION
BY LASER

Laser is short hand for Light Detection and Ranging or Laser Speed Measuring Device. Laser is similar to radar except instead of a radio signal it emits a beam of light. The device must meet the minimum design criteria for laser speed measuring devices. *Fla. Admin Code 15B- 2.014.*

The beam is actually three individual beams, and if directed incorrectly, the reading will be inaccurate. Since the beam is narrower than a radar signal, the tolerance for error by the operator increases. The device must be tested every six months for accuracy by a Florida registered professional engineer who has a FCC license. *Fla. Admin. Code 15B-2.016.*

This requires a certificate or document to be produced at the hearing. The device must be bench tested; meaning it must be removed from the vehicle for testing. In addition a written log must be maintained and contain an entry for accuracy checks performed at the beginning and end of each shift. *Florida Admin. Code 15B-2.015.*

A log means a document must be produced at the hearing. Failure by the state to produce means the case is dismissible. The operator must also pass a test to determine his/her ability to correctly operate the device and must produce a certificate to that effect.

PHOTO CITATIONS

Some municipalities issue citations based on a photograph of a vehicle passing a red light or speeding past a camera pre-set to trigger a photograph at a designated speed. The camera records the license plate and a citation is issued by mail to the registered owner of the vehicle. These tickets are invalid for many reasons. The driver may not be the registered owner and the alleged violator does not sign the citation and therefore has not promised to appear in court.

STOP LIGHT INFRACTIONS

A stop light statute usually reads as follows:

> *Vehicular traffic facing a steady red signal shall stop before entering the crosswalk on the near side of the intersection or, if none, then before entering the intersection and shall remain standing until a green indication is shown.*

A defense to this citation often depends upon the location of the officer who observed the alleged violation. Unless the officer was in a position to observe the light facing the vehicle he/she cannot testify to the condition of that light at the time the vehicle passed it.

It is not sufficient to presume the light was red if the officer observed the light facing him/her was green. Most traffic lights have shields that prevent observation of that light unless facing the light. The officer must be in a position to observe the light facing the driver. If the officer did not observe the light facing the vehicle then any testimony concerning the condition of the light is not admissible and an objection by the accused should be sustained and the case dismissed.

Traffic lights like any other mechanical or electrical device are subject to failure and malfunctioning from time to time and unless there is a maintenance record in court there is a legal presumption the light functioned properly unless there is competent evidence to the contrary. *Fla. Statute 316.074(5).*

Unless the officer checked the coordination of the traffic light after issuing the citation (which he/she most likely did not do) he/she cannot testify about the condition of the light facing the driver.

The next defense is whether the light was red when the vehicle passed it. The law allows a vehicle to enter the intersection on a yellow light and if while crossing the intersection the light turns red, it is not a violation. *Fla. Statute 316.075(2)(a)*

STOP SIGN INFRACTION

A stop sign statute generally requires a driver to stop at an intersection controlled by a stop sign at a clearly marked stop line. A citation issued for this offense is defended, as in other types of offenses, by what the officer was able to observe according to his location and ability to observe.

The stop line may have been eroded by time, weather and wear. The stop sign may have been obscured by growth of trees or obstruction or even partially bent out of view. A photograph of the condition of the sign is invaluable to the defense. A defense can also be made that the driver approaching the stop sign saw no on coming vehicles and therefore made the very briefest of stops that may not have been seen as a full stop by the officer.

A stop is all that the law requires; how brief the stop is <u>not</u> the issue.

The driver is usually in the best position to say if the car stopped by reason of the vehicle's reaction to the application of the brakes. The officer has no such advantage. Also the angle at which the officer observed the vehicle and for how long is also an issue to be exploited. If reasonable doubt is created concerning the stop that case should be dismissed. The standard of proof in all traffic cases is beyond a reasonable doubt. *Fla. Statute 318.14(6).*

POSSESSION OF OPEN CONTAINERS

A statute defining open containers will generally be as follows:

Possession of open containers of alcoholic beverages in vehicles prohibited.

As used in this section, "open container" means any container which is immediately capable of being consumed from, or the seal of which has been broken.

It is unlawful and punishable as provided in this section for any person to possess an open container or an alcoholic beverage while operating a vehicle in the state or while a passenger in or on a vehicle being operated in this state.

An open container shall be considered in the possession of the operator of a vehicle if the container is not in the possession of a passenger and is not located in a locked glove compartment, locked trunk, or other locked non passenger area of the vehicle.

An open container shall be considered to be in the possession of a passenger of a vehicle if the container is in the physical control of the passenger.

The elements of this offense are:
- That the officer must identify the person as a driver or passenger
- The container must be in the possession of that identified person

- The beverage must be alcoholic
- The beverage must be capable of being *immediately* consumed
- The beverage is not locked in glove compartment or trunk.

The best way to determine whether a beverage is alcoholic is a chemical analysis, not the opinion or the nose of the officer. Many sport utility vehicles, mini-vans and other vehicles do not have trunks or glove compartments large enough to hold containers. If the container is in a location that can reasonably be considered safe in a non-passenger area it should meet the requirements of the statute.

The officer must determine who had possession of the container, a driver or passenger. If the driver had no knowledge a passenger opened a container or removed it from a safe or locked place, then a reasonable doubt of guilt is raised.

The vehicle must be operated and not parked or standing without the engine running. If the officer stopped the vehicle for a different traffic violation and the container was not observable, a request to search the vehicle should be denied for lack of probable cause.

A search warrant signed by a judge is required before a legal search can be made without probable cause. Any evidence, material or object found as a result of an illegal search is not admissible in court as evidence against the accused.

TRAFFIC OFFENSE HEARING PROCEDURES

Non-judicial "hearing officers" and not judges now mostly conduct traffic hearings. Nevertheless they are empowered to conduct the hearing just like a judge.

The rules of evidence shall be liberally construed by the official hearing the case. *Fla. Rules of Traffic Court 6.460.* This means it should be liberally construed in favor of the defendant.

Arrive at the court early enough to locate the correct courtroom and to look at the court docket or calendar to locate your name. Sometimes things go wrong and the dockets are not correct. If your name does not appear just ask the court clerk to clear up the problem. Try to identify the officer who issued the ticket. His/her failure to appear is sufficient to dismiss the case. If the officer is present, ask to view his documents before the hearing so that you will not be under pressure in carefully examining the documents.

You are legally entitled to view the documents prior to the hearing. *Fla. Rules of Traffic Court 6.445.*

Be sure to dress properly (a suit and tie for men, or a dress or suit for women) as the court is sensitive on this matter. Arriving early will allow you time to listen to other cases and be familiar with the procedure as well as to gauge the judge's personality, demeanor and what the judge will or will not allow. When your name is called approach the podium and do not rest or lean upon it, stand erect and face the court. Remember the state always has the burden of proof and it must proceed first.

Have your list of essential documents as well as essential proof at hand.

Listen to the officer's testimony carefully and check off what he testifies to. When a document is offered examine it to see if it contains what is legally required. If it does not then "object" to the document on those grounds.

Do not interrupt the officer unless it is to object. When the officer has completed his/her testimony and offered all the documents it is your turn to "cross-examine" the witness. In doing so always be polite and respectful in asking questions and do not attack or impugn the witness. This can pay dividends later.

Ask the officer about the missing documents. When you have completed the cross-examination you can then "move" the court to dismiss the case on the grounds that the state has failed to prove a "prima facie" case. If your motion to dismiss is denied you then have the right to introduce whatever documents, witnesses or testimony in your defense.

You also have the right to make a "closing statement" in which you can sum up the reasons why the court should find you not guilty. *Fla. Rule 6.450(f).*

If the court, after all the evidence is introduced still finds you guilty there is a back-up position available. Ask the court to allow you to attend traffic school in lieu of a full fine, points against the license and adjudication of guilt. The court normally wants this request prior to trial to save the courts time but if you have conducted yourself properly and the court is impressed with your dress and demeanor the court may grant the request. Although microphones are displayed in court, many are not functional and there is no court record of the proceeding. Therefore if there is a finding of guilt and the accused wants to appeal the case, the accused must provide his/her own record of the case for the appellate court.

This can be done by taking a recording device to court to record the proceeding. *Fla. Rules of Traffic Court 6.460(b).*

The court should be asked at the start of the case whether there will be a court record of the hearing.

SUMMARY

Winning in traffic court requires a minimum of effort and understanding simple and uncomplicated legal methods. It is a system to force the state to meet its legal standards of proof. The court will not do this on behalf of the accused because it is not the court's function to defend or prosecute an accused. The accused must use the tools outlined in this booklet to make the state prove guilt. This can be accomplished by following these methods and procedures;

1.   Remain cool at the traffic stop.

2.   Obtain and read the statutory definition of the offense, element-by-element.

3.   If possible move the location of the place of hearing and the date.

4.   If the offense is a radar speed violation note all the necessary documents required and what constitutes a proper document as well as what oral proof is required. At the hearing make sure all the requirements are met by the state, element-by-element, document-by-document and all oral testimony.

5.   At the hearing; dress correctly and always be polite and respectful to the court and witnesses especially during cross-examination of the officer.

6.   Use language that is comfortable for you rather than trying to emulate a lawyer.

ABOUT THE AUTHOR

Seymour Stern is a practicing litigation lawyer for over forty years and has sat as a magistrate hearing traffic offense cases. His courtroom expertise as a judge and attorney l representing clients in traffic cases is the basis for the successful defense strategies and tactics outlined in this booklet. He has written articles on law published by the New York State Trial Lawyers Quarterly and republished by National Law Review and has lectured on law on behalf of the United States Foreign Consul.

www.ingramcontent.com/pod-product-compliance
Lightning Source LLC
Chambersburg PA
CBHW021939170526
45157CB00005B/2351